ADVENT FOR CHOIRS

COMPILED AND EDITED BY
MALCOLM ARCHER & STEPHEN CLEOBURY

MUSIC DEPARTMENT

OXFORD
UNIVERSITY PRESS

OXFORD
UNIVERSITY PRESS

Great Clarendon Street, Oxford OX2 6DP, England
198 Madison Avenue, New York, NY, 10016, USA

Oxford University Press is a department of the University of Oxford.
It furthers the University's aim of excellence in research, scholarship,
and education by publishing worldwide in

Oxford New York
Auckland Cape Town Hong Kong Karachi
Kuala Lumpur Madrid Melbourne Mexico City Nairobi
New Delhi Shanghai Taipei Toronto

With offices in

Argentina Austria Brazil Chile Czech Republic France Greece
Guatemala Hungary Italy Japan Poland Portugal Singapore
South Korea Switzerland Thailand Turkey Ukraine Vietnam

Oxford is a registered trade mark of Oxford University Press
in the UK and in certain other countries

© Oxford University Press 2000

The moral rights of the editors have been asserted

Database right Oxford University Press (maker)

First published 2000
First published in wiro binding 2006

5 7 9 10 8 6 4

ISBN 0–19–353025–2   978–0–19–353025–6 (pbk)
ISBN 0–19–335576–0   978–0–19–335576–7 (wiro)

Music and text origination by
Barnes Music Engraving Ltd., East Sussex
Printed in Great Britain on acid-free paper by
Halstan & Co. Ltd., Amersham, Bucks.

PREFACE

There has been a welcome awareness in recent times of the significance of the Advent period as distinct from that of Christmas. *Advent for Choirs* contributes to this by fulfilling the need in the Church for a comprehensive musical and liturgical resource for use both in carol services and throughout this rich and varied season.

This collection approaches Advent afresh, assembling 52 accessible pieces that span the whole gamut of periods, styles, and traditions. A wide selection of settings of the most important texts is included, many in new arrangements, and there are a number of specially commissioned works, including Bob Chilcott's 'Nova! nova!' and 'This is the record of John' by Grayston Ives.

Great care has been taken to offer pieces that will suit the needs and abilities of church, cathedral, and concert choirs. Repertoire that is widely available or particularly difficult has been avoided, and preference given instead to new and unjustly neglected music or works not easily available elsewhere. These include Lennox Berkeley's 'I sing of a maiden', Stephen Darlington's 'Jacob's Ladder', and Richard Lloyd's 'Drop down ye heavens'. An appendix at the back of the volume provides a list of repertoire not included in this volume for reasons of difficulty or because it is generally available.

Important liturgical texts such as the Advent Antiphons, Advent Prose, the Magnificat, Advent Wreath Prayers, and Prayer for the Blessing of Light are included here in new arrangements or editions. In addition to the traditional settings of the Matin and Vesper Responsories adapted from Palestrina, a new version of each by Gabriel Jackson is also included.

We have tried to make the book as easy to use and as versatile as possible. Pieces are presented alphabetically by title, and there is a list showing how the music relates to the most important Advent themes and readings. In addition, a succinct essay by The Very Reverend Michael Perham, a member of the Church of England Liturgical Commission, illuminates the meaning of Advent, its themes and traditions, and provides suggestions of how one might structure a service of readings and music. It is hoped that these features will assist clergy and musicians in choosing appropriate repertoire.

Our editorial aim has been to provide practical performing editions that are informed by current scholarship while remaining approachable by all choirs. Pieces with foreign language texts are given English singing translations wherever possible.

An opportunity has been taken to present the Advent Prose and Antiphons using more recent translations, and, in the case of the Antiphons, employing the Sarum version as a basis for the music. In order to fit English words to music originally composed for Latin texts, arbitrary decisions have necessarily been made in altering the music to yield satisfactory verbal stress. A very simple organ accompaniment has been provided, the only purpose of which is to facilitate tuning. These pieces are best performed unaccompanied.

We are very grateful to all those who have contributed to *Advent for Choirs* and especially to Mary Berry whose generous advice in the preparation of new plainsong editions has been invaluable. We hope that this book will inspire people to take an imaginative new look at the Advent season.

MALCOLM ARCHER
STEPHEN CLEOBURY
September 1999

CONTENTS

INDEX OF TITLES AND FIRST LINES

Where first lines differ from titles the former are shown in italics.
Pieces suitable for unaccompanied singing are marked thus *.

vi

THEMATIC INDEX OF MUSIC AND READINGS[†]

Where first lines differ from titles the former are shown in italics.
Pieces suitable for unaccompanied singing are marked thus *.

1. The Four Last Things
(death, judgement, hell, and heaven)

Readings
Job 19.21–7
Isaiah 25.6–9
Wisdom 3.1–9
Romans 8.14–23
2 Peter 3.8–15a
Revelation 21.22–22.5, 12–13
Matthew 25.1–13 *or* Matthew 25.31–end

Music

TITLE	COMPOSER / ARRANGER / EDITOR	NO.	PAGE
* Advent Prose (English)	ed. Cleobury	3a	11
* Advent Prose (Latin)	ed. Cleobury	3b	14
Advent Prose	Richard Lloyd	14	61
Creator of the stars of night	Malcolm Archer	13	56
Drop down, ye heavens	Richard Lloyd	14	61
* E'en So Lord Jesus, Quickly Come	Paul Manz	16	72
* Man, assay	Anon. Medieval English ed. Cleobury	28	127
* *Peace be to you and grace from him*	Paul Manz	16	72
* *Pour down, O heavens, from above*	ed. Cleobury	3a	11
* *Rorate caeli*	ed. Cleobury	3b	14
Veiled in darkness	G. L. Rudolph	47	199

2. The Coming of the King and the Kingdom

Readings
Samuel 7.1–11, 16
Isaiah 9.2–7
Jeremiah 23.5–6
Zechariah 9.9–10
Romans 12.1–2; 13.11–14
1 Thessalonians 5.16–24
Matthew 21.1–9 *or* Mark 13.24–37

Music

TITLE	COMPOSER / ARRANGER / EDITOR	NO.	PAGE
* *Blow ye the trumpet in Sion*	Francisco Guerrero ed. Morris	11	49
* Canite tuba	Francisco Guerrero ed. Morris	11	49
Creator of the stars of night	Malcolm Archer	13	56
How beautiful upon the mountains	John Stainer	19	87
How lovely are the messengers (from *Saint Paul*)	Felix Mendelssohn ed. Archer	20	92
* I look from afar	Gabriel Jackson	21	101
* *I look from afar*	G. P. da Palestrina ed. Cleobury	29	130
* Matin Responsory	G. P. da Palestrina ed. Cleobury	29	130
* Matin Responsory	Gabriel Jackson	21	101
O thou, the central orb	Charles Wood	34	149

[†]For a discussion of the significance of these Advent themes, please see the Liturgical Introduction (page xiii).

3. The Sin of Adam Reversed in the Birth of Christ

Readings

Genesis 3.1–20 *or* 8–15
Isaiah 64.1–9
Prayer of Manasseh
Romans 5.6–15
1 Corinthians 15.42–50
Galatians 4.1–7
John 3.16–21 *or* Luke 1.26–38

Music

4. The Witness of the Prophets

Readings

Isaiah 2.1–5
Isaiah 7.10–15
Isaiah 11.1–10
Micah 5.2–4
Malachi 4
2 Timothy 3.14–4.5
Luke 4.14–21 *or* Matthew 23.29–39

Music

5. Preparing for Christmas: Waiting and Expecting

Readings

Isaiah 35.1–10
Zechariah 2.10–end
Baruch 4.36–5.9
Philippians 4.4–9
1 Thessalonians 5.1–11
James 5.7–10
Matthew 24.36–44 *or* Luke 3.1–17

Music

TITLE	COMPOSER / ARRANGER / EDITOR	NO.	PAGE
* Advent Antiphons (English)	ed. Cleobury	*2a*	3
* Advent Antiphons (Latin)	ed. Berry	*2b*	8
* Come, thou Redeemer of the earth	German trad. arr. Cleobury	*12*	54
* *How shall I fitly meet thee* (from The *Christmas Oratorio*)	J. S. Bach ed. Archer	*51*	213
* *Judah and Jerusalem, fear not*	Gabriel Jackson	*46*	195
* *Judah and Jerusalem, fear not*	G. P. da Palestrina arr. Ledger	*48*	203
Let all mortal flesh keep silence	French carol arr. Cleobury	*25*	115
* Never weather-beaten sail	Richard Shephard	*30*	133
O come, O come Immanuel	15th cent. French arr. Rutter	*32*	141
O thou, the central orb	Charles Wood	*34*	149
* People look East	Besançon carol arr Ferguson	*35*	157
* Tomorrow go ye forth	Gabriel Jackson	*46*	195
* Vesper Responsory	G. P. da Palestrina arr. Ledger	*48*	203
* Vesper Responsory	Gabriel Jackson	*46*	195
* Wie soll ich dich empfangen (from The *Christmas Oratorio*)	J. S. Bach ed. Archer	*51*	213

6. John the Baptist

Readings

Judges 13.2–7, 24–25
Isaiah 40.1–11
Isaiah 61.1–4, 8–11
Malachi 3.1–6
Ecclesiasticus 48.1–10
Acts 13.14b–26
Luke 1.5–25 *or* Luke 1.57–66, 80

Music

TITLE	COMPOSER / ARRANGER / EDITOR	NO.	PAGE
Benedictus in C	C. V. Stanford	*9*	38
Blessed be the Lord God of Israel	C. V. Stanford	*9*	38
* Fuit homo missus a Deo	G. P. da Palestrina ed. Morris	*18*	79
* *Lo, there came a man, sent from God*	G. P. da Palestrina ed. Morris	*18*	79
On Jordan's bank	*Winchester New* arr. Archer	*33*	146
This is the record of John	Grayston Ives	*44*	187

7. Mary

(her conception, the annunciation to Mary and Joseph, and the visitation)

Readings

Samuel 2.1–10
Proverbs 8.22–31
Isaiah 61.10–62.3

Wisdom 9.1–12
Romans 5.12–21
Revelation 12.1–6
Luke 1.26–38 *or* Luke 1.39–49

Music

8.   Advent Antiphons

Readings

Ecclesiasticus 24.3–9   *O Sapientia* / O wisdom
Exodus 3.1–6   *O Adonaÿ* / O Lord of Lords
Isaiah 11.1–10   *O Radix Jesse* / O root of Jesse
Isaiah 22.21–23   *O Clavis David* / O key of David
Numbers 24.15–17   *O Oriens* / O morning star
Jeremiah 30.7–11a   *O Rex gentium* / O king of the nations
Matthew 1.18–23   *O Emmanuel* / O Emmanuel

Music

LITURGICAL INTRODUCTION

Celebrating Advent

Although one of the shortest seasons of the Christian year (never more than 28 days, and sometimes as few as 22), Advent is a rich and complex time, with huge potential to lead people into a deeper understanding of the Christian mysteries through its liturgy and music.

The coming of the Lord

At root, Advent is about preparing for the coming of the Lord. Both words—'preparing' and 'coming'—are important. Advent looks towards something yet to happen—the return of Jesus Christ at the end of time, the *Parousia*, as it is known by scholars, or 'the Second Coming', as people often say. The season is characterized by expectancy, hope (even longing), and by preparation. Throughout Advent are sung those wonderful hymns that invite 'Come, Lord, come', during which people may well picture the church decked out for Christmas and the baby in the crib, but this is not the true focus of the Advent hymns. For the hymn writers 'Come, Lord' invokes his return to judge.

This immediately presents us with a problem. For of all the teachings of the New Testament, the Second Coming is one of the most perplexing to the modern mind and some may be unconvinced by a literal proclamation that the end is near. But Christians in their different traditions have to wrestle with this talk of the 'end of time', and a variety of interpretations can be sustained whilst remaining true to the scriptures. What is quite certain is that they cannot simply abandon the whole world of 'eschatology'— the part of theology concerned with death and the final destiny of all things. Belief about the end of the present world order was so fundamental to Jesus Christ's own perception, and to his self-understanding, that a Christianity without it would be untrue to him and to the gospel. The period of Advent forces us to engage with the texts that speak of 'the end' and to wrestle with the concept that 'Christ will come again'. For this reason the 'four last things' (death, judgement, hell, and heaven) will always be among the proper themes of Advent and Christians should not ignore them.

The reality, however, is that the 'coming' for which people prepare will more often be the coming of Christmas, the annual celebration of a coming, once-upon-a-time, 'at Bethlehem of Judaea in the days of Herod the King'. This might seem to be a modern redesign of Advent, both because of our contemporary puzzlement about the Second Coming and because of the need to respond to the pressures of a secular and commercial Christmas. But the truth is that Advent has always had these two layers, a looking towards Christmas, *and* towards the Second Coming; liturgy is a discipline sufficiently subtle that its texts can hold the two together very satisfactorily and even creatively. Providing we do not lose sight of the 'Christ will come again' dimension, there is no harm (indeed positive good) in reflecting on it in parallel with preparations for the celebration of the First Coming at Bethlehem.

The structure of the season allows the emphasis to move from one dimension to the other on 17 December. Until 16 December, the liturgical provision focuses very much on the Second Coming, but from 17 December there starts a 'countdown to Christmas', the scripture readings taking us through the gospel material in Luke and Matthew that leads to the birth of Jesus.

These 'countdown' days are marked by special antiphons, often known as 'the great Os'. In origin, they are a series of antiphons to be sung before and after the Magnificat at Evening Prayer and, if used in that original way, they are still wonderfully appropriate today. Often known by their Latin names: *O Sapientia*, *O Adonai*, *O Radix Jesse*, *O Emmanuel*, etc. (which have almost become synonymous with the days themselves), they can, nevertheless, be sung or said in English. They are also often taken out of their original liturgical use and employed in Advent liturgies of different sorts and as introits and post-communions at the Eucharist. The antiphons are all woven into the familiar Advent hymn, 'O come, O come, Emmanuel', which, particularly in its seven-verse version, is little more than a metrical paraphrase. Those who use them should be aware of discrepancies of date. The medieval Sarum tradition inserted an additional Marian antiphon, *O Virgo virginum*, which was allocated to 23 December. This pushed all the other antiphons back a day, so that the sequence began on 16 December. In general, however, this Sarum sequence is not followed today and it is 17 December that marks the change of gear in Advent.

Sunday themes

The Sundays of Advent, and in particular their set scripture readings, do not necessarily follow this neat division of the season into two parts. The Roman Catholic Sunday Mass Lectionary and the Revised Common Lectionary, now establishing itself among churches in the West (including the Anglican Church), both focus on the Second Coming on the First Sunday of Advent. They introduce the figure of John the Baptist on the Second Sunday, stay with him on the Third, and devote the Fourth to the Annunciation / Visitation stories. This is a different programme to that in the *Book of Common Prayer*, for example, where John does not feature until the Third Sunday, but is retained for the Fourth Sunday, with no provision for the Annunciation / Visitation stories. There has also been a long tradition of 'Bible Sunday' being celebrated on the second Sunday of Advent. The theme ties in appropriately with the Advent emphasis on the Old Testament Scriptures. Nevertheless, there is a trend to move Bible Sunday to late October and this is where the new Anglican lectionary locates it. Those who choose music need to be aware of these differences.

Another sequence can find its way into the liturgy through the prayers at the lighting of the Advent 'wreath', 'ring', or 'crown'. (A version of the wreath is depicted on the cover of this book). Again, this has the 'countdown' element to it, with one more candle alight each successive Sunday until the fifth one, the Christmas candle, is lit on Christmas Day. There have been various attempts to identify each candle with a particular part of the preparation for Christmas, but there is no one universally agreed sequence of subjects. The one put forward in *The Promise of His Glory*, the Church of England's official service book for this season, gives the following sequence:

Advent 1:	The Patriarchs
Advent 2:	The Prophets
Advent 3:	John the Baptist
Advent 4:	Mary
Christmas Day:	Jesus Christ

This sequence sits quite happily alongside the lectionary provision, though its themes are not identical.

Does Advent liturgy have a distinctive character? The intention is that it should be marked by a restrained, joyful expectancy. In many places, it is customary to omit the *Gloria in Excelsis* at the Eucharist, so that this song of the angels comes back with particular appeal on Christmas night. There are few traditional texts used repeatedly throughout the season: there are the Advent Antiphons already mentioned; there is the Advent Prose (*Rorate caeli desuper*, or 'Pour down, O heavens, from above') but there is no tradition of omitting *alleluias* as is done in Lent, for Advent is not principally a penitential season. That element is not entirely missing, however; how could it be when the season bids Christians to reflect on the judgement of Christ? But what people often fail to comprehend is that from the New Testament onwards, the Church has looked upon the Coming of Christ not with fear, or seeking to put off the day, but with eager longing, expectation, and joy. It is this mood of 'sober joy' that the liturgy tries to capture. Preparation has an important place and penitence may be part of that preparation, but there is confidence and joy all the way through the season, with the sense that salvation is at hand, and a real yearning for the coming of the day of the Lord.

Special Advent services

For many churches and especially those with good musical resources, Advent has become a season for a special non-eucharistic liturgy. This might be better described as an extended Liturgy of the Word, perhaps with processional movements and stations (in a big church), and often with the use of darkness and light, sometimes built around the themes of the Advent Antiphons. Such a service—often called 'The Advent Carol Service'—has much to commend it, but the name has its problems. Most of the popular carols are essentially Christmas carols and one wants neither to anticipate Christmas on the First Sunday of Advent (sometimes as early as November), nor send people away dissatisfied and feeling cheated. Cathedrals tend to speak of 'The Advent Procession', but that implies space and a certain style which would not be appropriate in many parish settings. There is no one correct designation, but the matter needs careful reflection.

There are then further decisions to be made. The first relates to the shape of the service. Something along these lines would be appropriate in most settings:

- Kindling (and sharing) of light
- Greeting, introduction, and opening prayer
- Readings, with both silence and music between readings
- Gospel reading
- Intercession
- Lord's prayer
- Blessing

The music (instrumental or choral, and including psalmody and hymnody) links these elements of the service and provides the opportunity to reflect upon them.

Where there is opportunity for movement, whether by the ministers alone, the choir and ministers, or by the entire congregation, the order may well be dictated by the shape and furnishings of the building. A procession might simply move Eastwards through the church during the course of the service, with the sense of progressing on in pilgrimage to meet the Coming Lord. Alternatively, the liturgy might be gathered around the lectern for the reading of the Old Testament prophets, move to the font for the John the Baptist material, and on to the Lady Chapel for the Gospel of the Annunciation. There is no one set formula.

Another decision needs to be made in relation to darkness and light. The word 'candlelight' can be a powerful draw purely at the level of attracting a congregation, but there needs to be clear thinking about the purpose of the light and its symbolic use. Is the candlelight simply 'atmospheric'? Is the light (whether by candle or electricity) static, or is it moving through the church? If it is moving, what does it symbolize? Does the light stand for Christ 'who is our light' or are we investing it with some other meaning? When these questions have been clarified, there is the issue of whether 'darkness and light' should be the theme of the whole service, reflected in the readings and music, or whether it should provide a subtler message alongside another Advent theme. In general, there is a case for caution in developing the 'Light in the Darkness' theme, for it will feature prominently at the end of Epiphany in the celebration of Candlemas and is an essential element in the Easter Liturgy as well. Indeed, if an Advent Liturgy does opt to give darkness and light a high profile, consideration needs to be given to whether it should be as unlike, or as parallel to, the Easter Liturgy as possible. A case can be made for both.

Unless the theme is to be 'Light in the Darkness', then a theme, with appropriate readings, needs to be chosen. This book recognizes seven major Advent themes (which, of course, overlap extensively):

1. The Four Last Things
2. The Coming of the King and the Kingdom
3. The Sin of Adam Reversed in the Birth of Christ
4. The Witness of the Prophets
5. Preparing for Christmas: Waiting and Expecting
6. John the Baptist
7. Mary

Any of these would provide a suitable sequence of music and readings for Advent, although the latter ones would be rather more appropriate in the second part of the season than on the First Sunday of Advent. Of course, readings do not all need to be drawn from the scriptures, though non-biblical passages should always be selected with special care and should not be read from the lectern as if they were scripture. It should be made obvious to the listener that they are hearing something different. Nevertheless, as the tables of readings show, there is such a wealth of biblical material for use in Advent that one needs to be very convinced before reducing it to make room for other texts. Similarly, there is a case for the generous use of the Old Testament. The sequences of readings provided here assume four or five passages from the Old Testament, one or two from the Epistles or Revelation, and a single climactic one from the Gospels. The art is in finding the hymns and anthems that relate to the words and themes of the readings. Nothing should be arbitrary (nor need be).

It is not necessary to be too purist about themes. For instance, it may be right to devote most of the service to 'The Witness of the Prophets', focusing on the Old Testament passages that find an uncanny fulfilment in the birth of Christ, and yet choose the Annunciation Gospel, which points to Christmas, as the final reading. The aim is always to stimulate and lead on, but not to anticipate nor to arrive at Christmas too soon.

Texts for the spoken parts of an Advent service are not provided in this book, as individual denominations would choose to draw from their own sources. In the case of the Church of England, to do so would also duplicate the careful work undertaken by its Liturgical Commission in *The Promise of His Glory* (Church House Publishing & Mowbray, 1990, 1991). There, texts are provided for the Blessing and Sharing of Light, for introductions to the service, intercessions, and blessings, as well as a number of sequences of readings additional to those provided here.

A special service such as this, coming at the beginning of the season, establishes the distinctive character of Advent right from the start. This makes particular sense if the mood is maintained and developed. The special service is by no means as important as the careful choice of liturgical text and music week by week and day by day—a progression that builds on the season and its expectation. Adam, Jesse, David, Isaiah, Gabriel, John the Baptist, and Mary: they all have their place in leading us to Christmas Eve and to Jesus, the Lord for whose Coming Advent prepares us.

In *Advent for Choirs*, Malcolm Archer and Stephen Cleobury have provided the Church with a fine musical companion to the liturgy of Advent, with material that will both honour the tradition and provide new stimulus right throughout the season. There is much here for which to be grateful.

MICHAEL PERHAM
September 1999

for Mary

1. Adam lay ybounden

Words: 15th-century English

PHILIP LEDGER
(b. 1937)

[1] *Deo gracias!* = thanks be to God   [2] clerkes = clergy   [3] book = the Bible

This collection © Oxford University Press 2000

Printed in Great Britain

OXFORD UNIVERSITY PRESS, MUSIC DEPARTMENT, GREAT CLARENDON STREET, OXFORD, OX2 6DP

2a. Advent Antiphons (English)

The Promise of His Glory

edited by
Stephen Cleobury

1. *O wisdom*: December 17

O_____ wis- -dom, com-ing forth from the_ Most High, fill-ing_ all cre-a-tion and_ reign - ing to the ends of_ the earth;_ come_____ and teach_____ us_____ the__ way of truth.___

2. *O Lord of Lords*: December 18

O_____ Lord_____ of_ Lords, and ru-ler of the House of Is-ra-el,

A version of the Magnificat (in B flat) by Philip Moore, can be found on page 121 of this anthology.

* This cadence may be used at the end of each antiphon if preferred.

you ap - peared   to   Mo - ses   in   the   fire   of   the   burn - ing   bush,_____

and gave him the law on Si - na - i: come with your out - stretched arm_   and_ ran-som us. _____

3. *O root of Jesse*: December 19

Cantor   *Full*

O_____ root_ of_ Jes - se,   stand-ing as a sign a - mong_ the na - tions;

kings will keep si-lence be - fore_ you_____   for whom the na - tions long;_____

4. *O key of David*: December 20

5. *O morning star*: December 21

6. *O king of the nations*: December 22

cor - ner-stone, bind-ing all to - ge - ther: come and save___ the crea - ture

you___ fa - shioned___ from the dust__ of the earth.___

7. *O Emmanuel*: December 23

Cantor   *Full*

O___ Em - ma - nu - el,   our King and Law-giv-er, hope of_ the na - - tions

and_ their sa - viour:_   come___ and save___ us,___ O___ Lord our God.___

2b. Advent Antiphons (Latin)

(*The Great O Antiphons – Rite of Salisbury*)

Springfield Antiphonal*
edited by
Mary Berry

** 1. *O Sapientia*: December 17

VOICES

O_____ Sa - pi-én - ti - a, quæ ex o - re Al-tís-si-mi__ pro - dí-sti,

at - tín - gens a fi - ne u - sque ad fi-nem, fór - ti - ter:_____

su - á-vi-ter dis-po-né*ns*-que óm - ni - a: Ve -ni, a*d* do-cén-dum nos__ ví - am pru-dén-ti-æ.

2. *O Adonaÿ*: December 18

O_____ A - do - ná - ÿ, et dux do - mus__ Ís - ra - el,

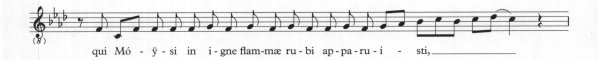

qui Mó - ÿ - si in i - gne flam-mæ ru - bi ap-pa-ru - í - sti,_____

et__ e-i in Sy-na le - gem de - dí - sti: Ve -ni, ad re - di - mén-dum nos__ in brá-chi-o__ ex -tén-to.

---

* ***Springfield Antiphonal**, c.*1300, CUL MS. Add.2602, fol. 12, *r,v.*
During modern repairs to the masonry, this manuscript fell from the rubble in the roof above the middle window in the south wall of the church. It is thought to have been hidden there by the two rectors, Alexander Gate and Thomas Marshall, in 1549.

** Read in reverse order, the initial letters of the seven great titles given to the long-awaited Messiah form two words: ERO CRAS – 'I shall be here tomorrow'.

† Here and elsewhere, wherever this note-form occurs, we have what is known as a 'liquescent note', which is hummed lightly on the consonant, on '*n*' or '*m*', etc., or simply softened whenever a different conjunction of consonants occures, such as 'd' 'd'.

3. *O Radix Jesse*: December 19

O———— Ra - dix— Jes - se,   qui stas in si-gnum po - pu - ló - rum,

su - per quem re-ges con-ti-né-bunt os— su - um,———   que*m* gen-tes de-pre - ca - bú*n*-tur:

Ve - ni ad li - be - rán - dum— nos,——— jam— no - li tar - dá - re.

4. *O Clavis David*: December 20

O———————— Cla - vis— Da - vid,   et sce-ptrum do - mus— Ís - ra - el,

qui á - pe-ris et ne-mo clau - dit,————   clau-dis et ne - mo— á - pé - rit:

Ve - ni, et e - duc vin - ctum de—— do - mo cár - ce - ris,

se - dén - tem— in té - ne - bris——— et— um - bra mor - tis.

5. *O Oriens*: December 21

O—— O - ri - ens, splen-dor lu - cis æ - tér-næ et sol ju-stí - ti - æ:————

Ve-ni, et— il - lú-mi - na se-dén-tem in té - ne - bris— et— u*m* - bra mor-tis.

6. *O Rex gentium*: December 22

O___ Rex gén-ti-um,   et de-si-de-rá-tus e - á - rum: la-pís-que an-gu-lá - ris, ___

qui fa-cis u - trá - que u - num: Ve - ni, sal - va hó - mi - nem, ___ quem de li - mo for-má-sti.

7. *O Emmanuel*: December 23

O___ Em-má-nu-el,   Rex et Lé-gi__ fer no-ster,   ex-pec-tá - ti - o gén-ti - um ___

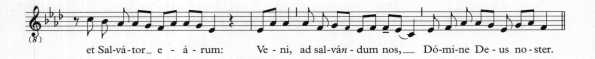

et Sal-vá-tor__ e - á - rum: Ve - ni, ad sal-ván - dum nos, ___ Dó-mi-ne De - us no-ster.

8. *O Virgo virginum**

O_____ Vir - go vír - gi - num,   quó - mo-do fi - et ___ i-stud:

qui-a ___ nec pri-mam sí-mi-lem vi-sa es, _____   nec ha-bé-re ___ se - quén-tem.

Fí - li - æ Je - rú - sa - lem,   quid me ___ ad-mi-rá - mi - ni?

di - ví-num est ___ my - sté - ri - um ___   hoc ___ quod cér - ni - tis.

* To the original series of seven antiphons, the rite of Salisbury added an eighth: *O Virgo virginum*. Because of this addition the whole series began one day earlier, on 16 December. (See the Liturgical Introduction.)

3a. Advent Prose (English)

The Promise of His Glory

edited by
Stephen Cleobury

* Verses may be sung by a soloist or semi-chorus.

3b. Advent Prose (Latin)

(*Rorate caeli*)

edited by
Stephen Cleobury

VOICES

Ro - rá - te cae - li dé - su - per___ et nu - bes plu - ant ju - stum.

1. Ne i - ra - scá - ris Dó - mi - ne, ne ul - tra me - mí - ne - ris in - i - qui - tá - tis:

ec - ce cí - vi - tas San - cti fa - cta est de - sér - ta: Si - on de - sér - ta fa - cta est:

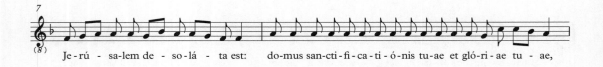

Je - rú - sa - lem de - so - lá - ta est: do - mus san - cti - fi - ca - ti - ó - nis tu - ae et gló - ri - ae tu - ae,

u - bi___ lau - da - vé - runt te pa - tres nos - tri.

2. Pec - cá - vi - mus, et fa - cti su - mus tam - quam im - mún - dus nos, et ce - cí - di - mus

qua - si fó - li - um u - ni - vér - si: et in - i - qui - tá - tes nos - trae qua - si ven - tus ab - stu - lé - runt nos:

14
(8) ab - scon - dí - sti fá - ci - em tu - am a no - bis,_____

15
(8) et al - li - sí - sti nos in ma - nu in - i - qui - tá - tis nos - trae.   *Refrain (Full)*

16
(8) 3. Vi - de__ Dó - mi - ne af - fli - cti - ó - nem pó - pu - li tu - i,   et mit - te quem mis - sú - rus es:

18
(8) e - mít - te A - gnum do - mi - na - tó - rem ter - rae,   de pe - tra de - sér - ti ad mon - tem fí - li - ae Si - on:

20
(8) ut áu - fe - rat ip - se ju - gum cap - ti - vi - tá - tis nos - trae.   *Refrain (Full)*

21
(8) 4. Con - so - lá - mi - ni,   con - so - lá - mi - ni,   pó - pu - le me - us:

22
(8) ci - to vé - ni - et sa - lus tu - a: qua - re moe - ró - re__ con - sú - me - ris,

24
(8) qui - a in - no - vá - vit te__ do - lor? Sal - vá - bo te,   no - li ti - mé - re,___

27
(8) e - go__ e - nim sum Dó - mi - nus De - us tu - us, San - ctus Is - ra - el, re - dém - ptor tu - us.   *Refrain (Full)*

4. Advent Wreath Prayers

The Promise of His Glory

MALCOLM ARCHER
(b. 1952)

The quasi-plainsong sections should be sung freely and with flexibility. The chanted sections should follow the natural word stresses and are akin to the style of Anglican Chant.

Advent 2

that we may be found ready
    and watching when he comes a-gain   in   glory   and judgement;

Cantor

for   you are our light and our sal - va - tion.   Bless-ed be God___ for__ ev - er.

Advent 3

Cantor   *Full*

Bless-ed are you,_____   Sov-reign Lord,   just_____   and_

true: to   you_ be praise__ and glo - ry for__ ev - er!

Your prophet John the Baptist was witness to the truth   as a   burning and shi-ning light.

May we your servants rejoice in his light, and so be led to witness to him who is the

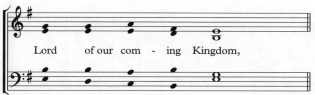

Lord of our coming Kingdom,

Cantor Je-sus our Sa-viour and King of the a-ges. *Full* Bless-ed be God for ev-er.

Advent 4

Cantor Bless-ed are you, Sov-reign Lord, *Full* mer-ci-ful and

gen-tle: to you be praise and glo-ry for ev-er!

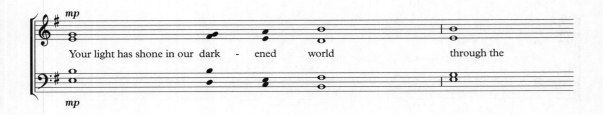

Your light has shone in our dark - ened world   through the

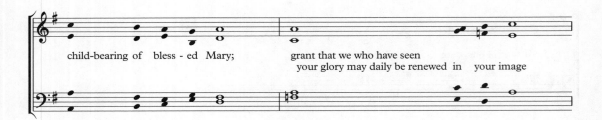

child-bearing of bless - ed Mary;   grant that we who have seen
your glory may daily be renewed in   your image

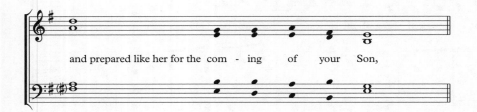

and prepared like her for the com - ing   of   your   Son,

Cantor

who is the Lord____ and Sa-viour of all.   Bless-ed be God____ for__ ev - er.

Christmas Day

Cantor

Bless-ed are you,_____ Sov-reign Lord,   King_____ of__

Peace: to you__ be praise__ and glo - ry for__ ev - er!

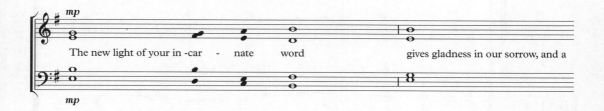

The new light of your in -car - nate   word   gives gladness in our sorrow, and a

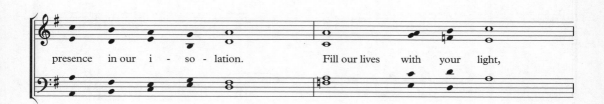

presence   in our i - so - lation.   Fill our lives   with   your   light,

until they over - flow   with   gladness   and   praise.

Cantor

Je - sus our Sa - viour and King of the a - ges.   Bless-ed be God__ for__ ev - er.

5. Alma redemptoris mater

Words: Medieval English

ANON. (Medieval)
edited by
Stephen Cleobury

[1] *Alma redemptoris mater* = Mother redemptress [2] Anon = straightway; forthwith [3] rood = crucifix [4] pight = pitched

The order of performance is: Refrain, Verse 1; Refrain, Verse 2; etc. The piece ends with the refrain. It may be effective for the whole choir to sing the refrain and for the verses to be taken by a pair of soloists. If a shorter version is needed, the refrain could be omitted after verses 1–4.

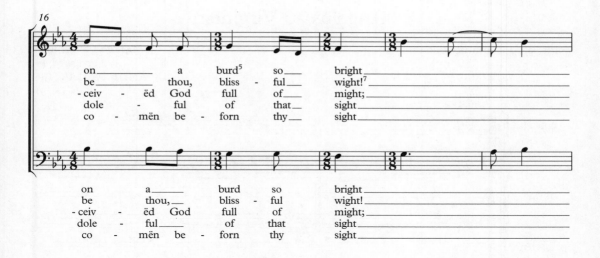

on _____ a burd[5] so ____ bright_____
be_____ thou, bliss - ful____ wight!\[7]_____
- ceiv - ëd God full of____ might;_____
dole - ful of that____ sight_____
co - mën be - forn thy____ sight_____

on _____ a_____ burd so _____ bright_____
be_____ thou,____ bliss - ful wight!_____
- ceiv - ëd God full of might;_____
dole - ful of that sight_____
co - mën be - forn thy sight_____

_____ that men cle-pen[6] Ma - ry,____ full____ of____ might,
_____ To ben cle-pëd[8] now_____ art____ thou____ dight[9]
_____ Then men wist[10] well_____ that____ she____ hight[11] } re -
_____ Till she see____ him rise____ up - right,
_____ With that bur - dë that____ is____ so____ bright,

_____ that men cle - pen Ma - ry,____ full____ of____ might,
_____ To ben cle - pëd now_____ art____ thou____ dight
_____ Then men wist____ well_____ that____ she____ hight } re -
_____ Till she see____ him rise____ up - right,
_____ With that bur - dë that____ is____ so____ bright,

D.C.

- demp - to - ris_____ ma - - - ter._____

[5] burd = lady; maiden [6] clepen = call [7] wight = person; human being [8] clepëd = called [9] dight = appointed [10] wist = know
[11] hight = named

to Philip Ledger and the choir of King's College, Cambridge

6. Angelus ad Virginem

Words: late 13th-century English

Melody: 13th century
arranged by
ANDREW CARTER
(b. 1939)

Translation

1. The angel, coming secretly to the Virgin, calming the Virgin's fear, said: 'Hail! Mary, Queen of Virgins! You shall conceive the Lord of Heaven and Earth and give birth, remaining a virgin, to the Salvation of mankind; you, made the Gateway of Heaven, the cure for sin.'
2. 'How shall I conceive, since I know not a man? How shall I break what I have resolutely vowed?' 'The grace of the Holy Spirit shall perform all this. Fear not, but rejoice, confident that chastity will remain pure in you by the power of God.'
3. At this, the noble Virgin, replying, said to him: 'I am the humble servant of almighty God. To you, heavenly messenger, who know so great a secret, I give my assent and desire to see done what I hear, and ready to obey God's will.'
4. O Mother of the Lord, who restored peace to angels and men when you gave birth to Christ, beg of your Son that he may show himself favourable to us and wipe away our sins, offering help to enjoy the blessed life after this exile.

(The editors of *The New Oxford Book of Carols*)

CHOIR 2 (melody)

4. E - ia Ma - ter Do - mi - ni, Quae pa - cem red - di -

CHOIR 1

Ah

Add

-dis - ti   An - ge - lis et ho - mi - ni, Cum Christ - um ge - nu -

ah

-is - ti;   Tu - um ex - o - ra Fi - li - um

ah

+ Reed

Bishopthorpe, December 1980

7. A tender shoot

English text by
William Bartholomew

OTTO GOLDSCHMIDT
(1829–1907)

For the people of St John the Baptist, Tisbury, past and present,
as they celebrate the 700th Anniversary of their Lady Chapel, 1999

8. Ave Maria

The Angelic Salutation

MALCOLM ARCHER
(b. 1952)

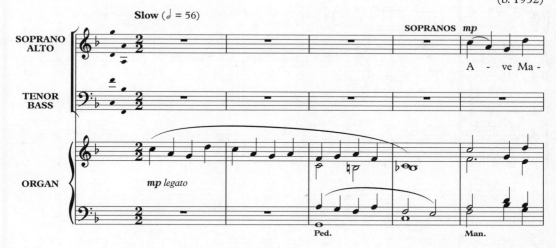

Translation

Hail, Mary, full of grace, the Lord is with you.
Blessed are you among women, and blessed is the fruit of your womb, Jesus.
Holy Mary, Mother of God, pray for us sinners now and at the hour of our death.
Amen.

et__ be-ne - dic -tus, et__ be-ne - dic-tus fruc-tus ven-tris tu — i

Man. Ped.

Je — sus. A - ve Ma -

-ri - a gra - ti - a ple - na__ Do - mi-nus te - cum__

be - ne - dic-ta tu__ in mu-li - e - ri - bus__

Ped.

et be-ne- dic - tus,__ et be-ne - dic - tus__ fruc-tus ven-tris tu - i__

Je - - sus.__

SOPRANOS (semi-chorus)

S. Sanc -ta Ma - ri - a__ Ma - ter__ De - i__

TENORS

T. Sanc -ta Ma - ri - a Ma - ter__ De - i o - ra pro

Man.

Ped.

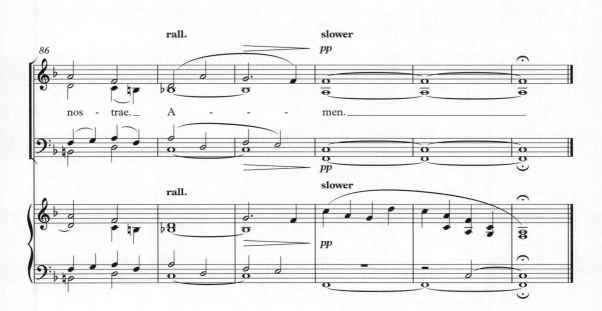

9. Benedictus in C

Luke 1: 68–79

C. V. STANFORD
(1852–1924)

to Stephen Cleobury and King's College Choir, Cambridge

10. Bogoroditsye Dyevo

(*Mother of God and Virgin*)

Words from the Liturgy of Vespers

ARVO PÄRT
(b. 1935)

English version

Virgin Mother of God,
Hail, Mary, full of grace, the Lord is with you.
Blessed are you among women, and blessed is the fruit of your womb,
for you gave birth to the saviour of our souls.

Advice on the pronunciation of Russian transliterations is given on page 48.

chrye - va Tvŏ - ye - - go,   ya - ko Spa-ssa rŏ-di - la ye-ssi-dush na - shikh,

S. ya - ko Spa-ssa rŏ-di - la ye-ssi dush na - shikh.

A. ya - ko Spa-ssa rŏ-di - la ye-ssi dush na - shikh.

T. ya - ko Spa-ssa rŏ-di - la ye-ssi dush na - shikh.

B. ya - ko Spa-ssa rŏ-di - la ye-si dush na - shikh.

*

S.
A. Bŏ-gŏ - ro-di-tsye Dye-vo, ra - dui-ssya, Bla-gŏ - dat-na - ya Ma - ri-ye, Go -

T.
B.

* Keyboard reduction for rehearsal purposes only.

- spod (s)Tŏ - bo - yu.   Bla - gŏ - slŏ - vyen - na   Tyi vzhe - nakh, i   bla - gŏ - slŏ - vyen Plod

più lento   rit.

chrye - va   Tvŏ - ye - go,   ya - ko Spa - ssa rŏ - di - la ye - ssi dush na - shikh.

Russian transliterations

Those who have never sung in Russian using a phonetic spelling of the Cyrillic alphabet should not be discouraged from attempting it. In fact, Russian sounds are surprisingly similar to those found in English (though the vowels are largely Italianate), and no attempt at an 'accent' is necessary. Some choirs may be fortunate enough to have a Russian speaker among their members or friends, who can help to perfect what a transliteration can only broadly suggest. The following remarks have therefore been kept to a minimum in the hope that the undertaking will not appear too daunting.

1. The most 'foreign' sound in Russian is the so-called 'hard i'. Here it is represented by 'yi'. This is pronounced not forward, like the usual English 'i', but backward with an almost adenoidal sound. The main thing is to avoid pronouncing 'yi' as the usual 'i'; try to keep it dark and covered.

2. Clusters of consonants can look intimidating but need not be so. The sound 'kh' is the guttural 'ch' as found in the Scottish word 'loch'; 'zh' is the voiced version of 'sh' and sounds as the 'j' in French 'je'; 'shch' sounds as in 'English church'.

3. The letter 'o' in a pre-stressed syllable (shown in this book as ŏ) is so modified and lightened that it is best pronounced as an 'a'. The letter 'o' in any other unstressed position is pronounced like the 'a' in 'sofa'.

4. Some Russian words, usually verbs, end with a 't' followed by a 'soft sign'. This so softens the 't' that in practice it sounds like 'ts', as in 'rabbits'. In such cases the 's' is shown in brackets. Otherwise, soft signs in Russian have been ignored as most English speaking is soft anyway.

5. The letter 's' in the middle of words has usually been represented by 'ss' in order to prevent it being mispronounced as a 'z' (i.e. 'Mussorgsky' and not the regularly mispronounced 'Muzorgsky').

David Lloyd-Jones

11. Canite tuba

(*Blow ye the trumpet*)

Joel 2: 1; Isaiah 11: 4

FRANCISCO GUERRERO (1528–99)
edited by
Timothy Morris

All dynamics are editorial.

12. Come, thou Redeemer of the earth

St Ambrose
translation by J. M. Neale
and others

German traditional melody: adapted by
MICHAEL PRAETORIUS (1571–1621)
arranged by
STEPHEN CLEOBURY (b. 1948)

This arrangement can be performed in several ways to suit particular circumstances: *a)* with organ accompaniment throughout, the organ doubling the voices in verses 2–7, *b)* unaccompanied throughout, and *c)* SATB throughout, using the harmony of verse 2, with or without organ doubling.

A version of the Matin Responsory, can be found on page 130 of this anthology.

for Dr Richard Seal and the Salisbury Diocesan Choirs

13. Creator of the stars of night

Office Hymn
English text by J. M. Neale
and editors of *The New English Hymnal*

MALCOLM ARCHER
(b. 1952)

The — Son of — Man, yet — all — di - vine. _____

shrine, The — Son of — Man, yet — all — di - vine. _____

3. At thy great name, — ex - alt - ed now,   All knees must bend, — all   hearts must bow,

Ah _____   ah _____

Ah _____   ah _____

And things in heav'n and   earth shall own   That — thou — art   Lord and   King a -

_____   ah _____   ah _____

_   ah _____   ah _____

ah _____

glo - ry be From age to age e - ter - nal -

From age to age e - ter - nal - ly.

ff   *poco a poco dim.*

unis.   *mp*

- ly.   A - men,   A -

mp

A - men,   A -

Sw.

p   *pp*   *a niente*

A - men,   A - men.

p   *pp*   *a niente*

- men,   A - men,   A - men.

pp   *a niente*

32'

14. Drop down, ye heavens

The Advent Prose

RICHARD LLOYD
(b. 1933)

* 2 Sopranos and 1 Alto on each side sing words: remainder hum (closed lips).

* This held organ chord to cease on the rest between 'righteousness' and 'let the earth'.

15. Ecce concipies

(Behold, thou shalt conceive)

Luke 1: 31–3

JACOB HANDL (1550–91)
edited by
Timothy Morris

All dynamics are editorial.

SECUNDA PARS

SECUNDA PARS

to John

16. E'en So Lord Jesus, Quickly Come

Revelation 22
adapted by Ruth Manz

PAUL MANZ
(b. 1919)

17. Es ist ein Ros' entsprungen

(A rose there is a-springing)

English text by Donald Cashmore

arranged by
DONALD CASHMORE (*v.*2 & 3)
(b. 1926)
and MICHAEL PRAETORIUS (*v.*1)
(1571–1621)

* Keyboard reduction for rehearsal only.

18. Fuit homo missus a Deo

(Lo, there came a man, sent from God)

Based on John 1: 6–8

G. P. da PALESTRINA
(*c.*1525–94)
edited by
Timothy Morris

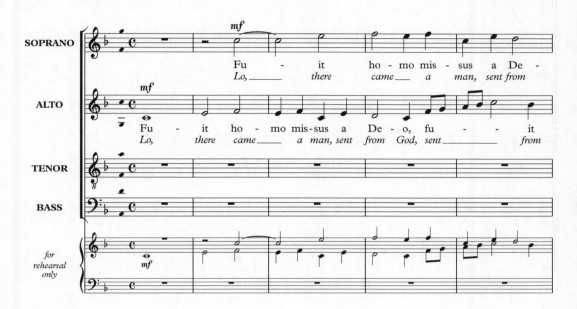

All dynamics are editorial.

19. How beautiful upon the mountains

Isaiah 52: 7

JOHN STAINER
(1840–1901)

peace;   that   pub - lish - eth   sal - va - tion,   that

moun - tains   are the   feet of him that bring-eth good   ti - dings,   that

mf

How

pub - lish - eth   peace,   that

pub - lish - eth   peace;   that   pub - lish - eth   sal - va - tion.

mf

How

beau - ti-ful up-on the   moun - tains are the feet of him that bring-eth good   ti - dings,

moun - tains, how beau - ti - ful the feet of

How beau - ti - ful up-on the moun - tains the feet of

How beau - ti - ful up-on the

How beau - ti - ful the feet of

Ped.

him that bring-eth good ti - dings, that pub - lish-eth peace, peace.

him that bring-eth good ti - dings, that pub - lish-eth peace, peace.

moun-tains that bring-eth good ti - dings, that pub - lish-eth peace, peace.

him, how beau - ti - ful up-on the moun-tains, that pub - lish-eth peace, peace.

rall.

20. How lovely are the messengers

From *Saint Paul*
Romans 10: 15, 18

FELIX MENDELSSOHN
(1809–47)
edited by
Malcolm Archer

preach____ us the gos-pel of peace!   How love -

preach us the gos-pel of peace!   How love - ly are   the   mes - sen - gers   that

To   all____   the

- ly   are they   that preach us the gos-pel of   peace! To all   the

To   all____   the

preach us the gos-pel of   peace,   the   gos - pel   of peace! To all   the

cresc.

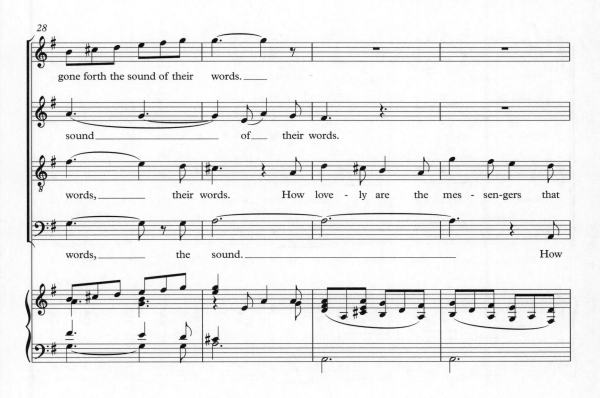

gone forth the sound of their words.___

sound_____ of___ their words.

words,_____ their words. How love - ly are the mes - sen - gers that

words,_____ the sound._____ How

How love - ly are the mes - sen - gers that preach us the gos-pel of

How love - ly are the mes - sen - gers that preach us, that

preach us the gos-pel of peace, the mes - sen - gers that preach us, that

love - ly are the mes - sen - gers, the mes - sen - gers that preach

all the lands their glad ti - dings.
all the lands their glad ti - dings. How love - ly are the
all the lands their glad ti - dings.____
all the lands their glad ti - dings.____

dim.
p

How love - ly____ they that
mes - sen-gers that preach us the gos-pel of peace! How love - ly are the mes - sen -
How love - ly they that
How love - ly they that

Commissioned by Stephen Darlington and the Choir of Christ Church Cathedral, Oxford,
with funds provided by Southern Arts.

21. I look from afar

Matin Respond
Advent Sunday

GABRIEL JACKSON
(b. 1962)

* Keyboard reduction for rehearsal only.
The companion Vesper Respond 'Tomorrow go ye forth', also by Gabriel Jackson, is found on page 195 of this anthology.

22. I sing of a maiden

Words: 15th-century English

LENNOX BERKELEY
(1903–89)

Slow

SOPRANO
ALTO

1. I   sing   of   a   maid - en
2. He   came   all   so   still - ë
3. He   came   all   so   still - ë
4. He   came   all   so   still - ë
5. Moth - er   and   maid - en   Was

TENOR
BASS

That   is   mak - ë - less:[1]   King   of   all
There[3]   his   moth - er   was,   As   dew   in   Ap -
To   his   moth - er's   bow'r,   As   dew   in   Ap -
There   his   moth - er   lay,   As   dew   in   Ap -
ne - ver   none   but   she;   Well   may   such   a

D.C.

king - ës   To   her   son   she   ches.[2]
- ril - lë   That   fall - eth   on   the   grass.
- ril - lë   That   fall - eth   on   the   flow'r.
- ril - lë   That   fall - eth   on   the   spray.
la - dy   God - dës   moth - er   be.

Dynamics at performers' discretion.

[1] makeless = matchless; unmated   [2] ches = chose   [3] There = where

23. Jacob's Ladder

Traditional

STEPHEN DARLINGTON
(b. 1952)

* To perform this piece successfully, it is necessary for the lower parts to stagger their breathing throughout.

pil - low he lay;   He__ saw in a vi - sion a lad - der so high, That its
not yet de-cayed;   Ma - ny mil - lions have climbed it and reach'd Si - on's hill, And__
guard - ing it still: And re - mem - ber, each step that by faith we pass o'er, Some
hith - er, ye blest,   Here are re - gions of light, here are man - sions of bliss.' O,__

ah_____   ah____

foot was on earth and its top in the sky.
thou - sands by faith are__ climb - ing it still.
pro - phet or mar - tyr hath trod it be - fore.
who would not climb such a lad - der as this?

S. TUTTI

A - le - lu - ia to Je - sus whose

ah_____

ah_____

(ah)_____   ah____

ah_____

birth sets us free And hath raised up a lad - der of mer - cy for me, And hath raised up a lad - der of

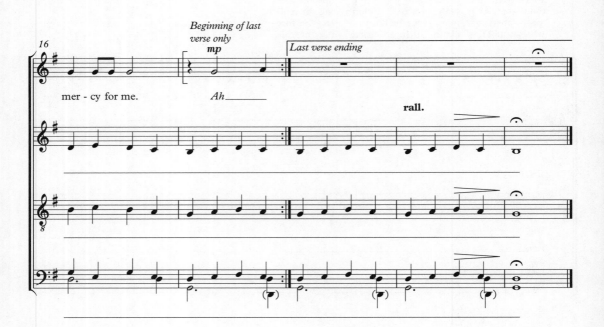

mer - cy for me.   Ah_____

24. Jesus Christ the Apple Tree

Words from *Divine Hymns or*
Spiritual Songs, compiled by
Joshua Smith

ELIZABETH POSTON
(1905–87)

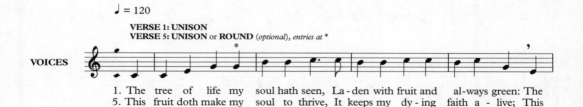

1. The tree of life my soul hath seen, La - den with fruit and al - ways green: The
5. This fruit doth make my soul to thrive, It keeps my dy - ing faith a - live; This

tree of life my soul hath seen, La - den with fruit and al - ways green:
fruit doth make my soul to thrive, It keeps my dy - ing faith a - live;

straight on for v. 2
v. 5: **Fine**

The trees of na - ture fruit - less be Com - pared with Christ the ap - ple tree.
Which makes my soul in haste to be With Je - sus Christ the ap - ple tree.

S.S.A.A. unaccompanied or S.(S.) acc.

2. His beau - ty doth all things ex - cel: By faith I know, but ne'er can tell, His

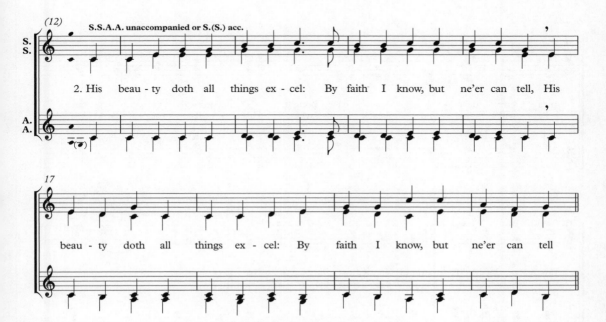

beau - ty doth all things ex - cel: By faith I know, but ne'er can tell

* In accompanied performance it may prove effective for the 'optional ending' at the foot of the next page to be played after verse 5.

(20) cresc.   *straight on for vv. 3 & 4*

The glo - ry which I now can see In Je - sus Christ the ap - ple tree.

cresc.

(24)   **4-PART**, or **UNISON (acc.)**

S. A.

3. For hap - pi - ness I long have sought, And plea - sure dear - ly
4. I'm wea - ry with my for - mer toil, Here I will sit and

T. B.

28

I have bought: For hap - pi - ness I long have sought, And
rest a - while: I'm wea - ry with my for - mer toil, Here

31

plea - sure dear - ly I have bought: I missed of all; but
I will sit and rest a - while: Un - der the sha - dow

34   *after v. 4:* **D.C.** *for v. 5* | *optional ending*
                                                                               last time (acc. only)

now I see 'Tis found in Christ the ap - ple tree.
I will be, Of Je - sus Christ the ap - ple tree.

25. Let all mortal flesh keep silence

Liturgy of St James
translation by Gerard Moultrie

French carol
arranged by
STEPHEN CLEOBURY
(b. 1948)

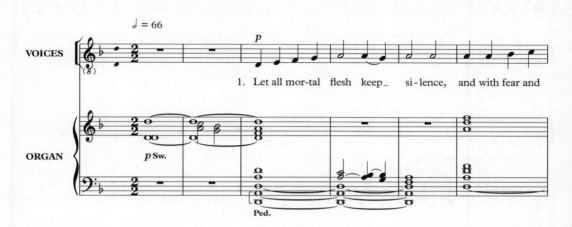

2. King of Kings, yet born of__ Ma - ry, as of old on earth he__ stood, Lord of lords, in hu - man ves - ture— in the bo-dy and the__ blood— He will give to all the faith - ful his own self for heaven - ly__ food.

3. Rank on rank the

* In verse 2 the tied semibreves may be played on pedal 8′ only, freeing the left hand to double the voices, perhaps with a sesquialtera registration.

host of__ hea - ven spreads its van-guard on the__ way, As the Light of

light de - scend - eth from the realms of end - less__ day, That the powers of

hell may van - ish as the dark-ness clears a - way.

SOPRANO DESCANT   *f*

S.

4. At his feet the six - winged__ se - raph;

ALL OTHER VOICES   *f*

(8)

4. At his feet the six - winged se - raph;

cresc.   **più **f***

Man.   Ped.

* In verse 4 the left hand could be played on a reed stop (in which case, omit bracketed notes in first bar).

26. Long ago, prophets knew

Fred Pratt Green

Melody: Piae Cantiones 1582
arranged by
MALCOLM ARCHER
(b. 1952)

Unison *f* 1. Long a - go, pro - phets knew Christ would come, born a Jew, Come to make all things new; Bear his

S. & A. *mf* 2. God in time, God in man, This is God's time - less plan: He will come, as a man, Born him -

T. & B. *mf* 3. Ma - ry, hail! Though a - fraid, She be - lieved, She o - beyed. In her womb God is laid: Till the

Unison *f* 4. Jour - ney ends! Where a - far Beth - lem shines, like a star, Sta - ble door stands a - jar. Un - born

22

Peo - ple's bur - den,   Free - ly love and par - don.
-self of wo - man,   God di - vine - ly hu - man.
time ex - pect - ed,   Nur - tured and pro - tect - ed,
Son of Ma - ry,   Sa - viour, do not tar - ry!

Ring, bells,

30

ring,   ring,   ring!   Sing, choirs, sing,   sing,   sing!

37   *D.C.*

When he comes,   when he comes,   Who will make him wel - come?
(v.4) Je - sus comes!   Je - sus comes!   We will make him wel - come!

(♯ *last time only*)

Ped.

27. Magnificat in B flat

(*Third Service*)

Canticle of the B. V. M.
(Luke 1: 46–55)

PHILIP MOORE
(b. 1943)

* Plainsong passages can be performed with a variety of forces (semi-chorus, solo, full, or an alternation of any of these). It is left to the imagination of the director to choose the most suitable scheme.
The Plainsong should be sung with freedom. There should be no breaks between sections in the organ part.
A version of the Advent Antiphons in English can be found on page 3 of this anthology.
The original version of this piece, scored for ATB, is distributed by Cathedral Music.

him: through - out all gen - er - a - tions.

fear_____ him: through - out all gen - er - a - tions.

fear him: through - out all_____ gen - er - a - tions.

them that fear him: through - out all gen - er - a - tions.

dim.

He hath shewèd strength with his arm:

Man.

in tempo

he hath scatterèd the proud in the imagina - tion of their hearts.

28. Man, assay

Words: Medieval English

ANON. (Medieval)
edited by
Stephen Cleobury

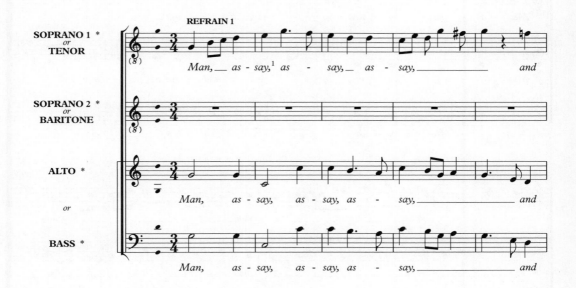

[1] *assay* = attempt to endeavour

* This piece can be performed using either S.S.A. or T.Bar.B. voice groups.

The order of performance is: Refrain 1, Refrain 2, Verse 1; Refrain 1, Refrain 2, Verse 2; etc. The piece ends with the refrains.
It may be effective for the whole choir to sing the refrains and for the verses to be taken by a pair of soloists. If a shorter version is
needed, the second refrain could be omitted after verses 1–3.

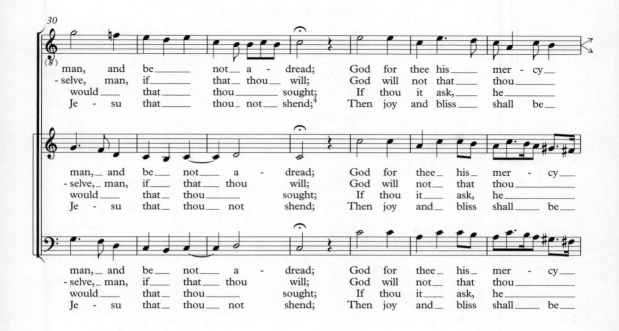

[2]spill = perish [3]nays it nought = negates (your sins) and sets (them) at nothing [4]shend = be punished for your deeds

29. Matin Responsory

adapted from a Magnificat by
G. P. da PALESTRINA (*c*.1525–94)
edited by
Stephen Cleobury

Italicized syllables should be lengthened slightly. A small break should be made at vertical lines in the text.

Second SOPRANO SOLO

Hear, O thou Shepherd of
Israel, | thou that leadest } Jo-seph like a sheep, —

should_____ come?

Tell us,   art thou   he   that   should_____ come?_____

should_____ come?

FULL SOPRANOS

Stir up thy strength,   O Lord, and come___

peo - ple   Is - ra - el.

to *reign* over thy   peo - ple___   Is - ra - el.___
peo - ple   Is - - - ra - el.

peo - ple   Is - ra - el.___

CANTOR

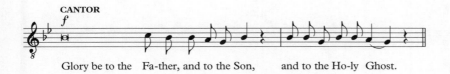

Glory be to the Fa-ther, and to the Son,   and to the Ho-ly Ghost.

FULL MEN

An arrangement of 'Come, thou Redeemer of the earth' by Stephen Cleobury can be found on page 54 of this anthology.

30. Never weather-beaten sail

Thomas Campion

RICHARD SHEPHARD
(b. 1949)

For David Hill and The Bach Choir
in celebration of the 80th Birthday of Sir David Willcocks

31. Nova! nova!

Words: 15th-century (modernized)

BOB CHILCOTT
(b. 1955)

[1] *Nova! nova! 'Ave' fit ex 'Eva'.* = News! news! 'Ave' is made from 'Eva'.

32. O come, O come Immanuel

18th-century Latin
translation by J. M. Neale
and others

Melody: 15th-century French
adapted and arranged by
JOHN RUTTER (b. 1945)

This arrangement is scored for 2 oboes, 2 horns, organ (opt.), and strings; scores and instrumental parts are available on hire.

33. On Jordan's bank

Charles Coffin
translated by John Chandler
and the editors of *Hymns & Psalms*

Melody: Winchester New
arranged by
MALCOLM ARCHER
(b. 1952)

1. On Jordan's bank the Baptist's cry
2. Then cleansed be ev-'ry Chris-tian breast,

An-noun-ces that the Lord is nigh; A-wake and hear-ken,
And fur-nished for so great a guest! Yea, let us each our

after v.2: straight on for v.3

for he brings Glad ti-dings from the King of kings!
heart pre-pare For Christ to come and en-ter there.

34. O thou, the central orb

H. R. Bramley

CHARLES WOOD
(1866–1926)

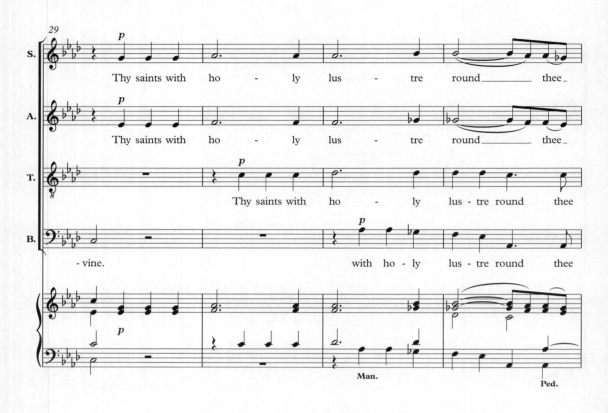

* Some scholars have suggested that 'day' is a misreading of the word 'clay' in the original manuscript. ('Clay' would seem to make more sense in the context of this passage.)   (The Editors)

35. People look East

Eleanor Farjeon

Melody: Besançon carol
arranged by
BARRY FERGUSON (b. 1942)

1. Peo-ple look East. The time is near_ Of the crown-ing of_ the

year. Make your house fair as you_ are a - ble, Trim the hearth and set_ the

ta - ble. Peo-ple look East, and sing to - day: Peo-ple look East, to - day:_ Love the Guest is on_ the

way. 2. Fur-rows, be glad. Though earth is bare, One more seed_ is plant - ed

there:___ Give up your strength to nour - ish, That in course the flow'r may

there: Give up your strength the seed to nour - ish, That in course the flower may

there:___ Give up your strength to nour - ish, That in course the

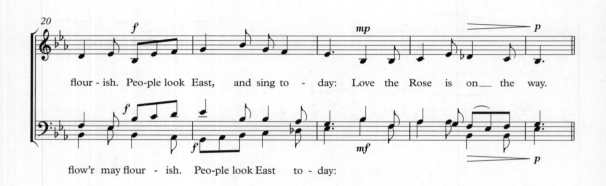

flour - ish. Peo-ple look East, and sing to - day: Love the Rose is on__ the way.

flow'r may flour - ish. Peo-ple look East to - day:

SOPRANOS
mf bright tone

3. Stars, keep the watch. When night is dim One more light the bowl__ shall

brim, Shin-ing be - yond the fros - ty wea - ther, Bright as sun__ and moon to -

-ge - ther. Peo-ple look East, and sing to - day: Love the Star is on__ the way.

4. An-gels, an - nounce to man__ and beast__ Him who com - eth from__ the

East. Set ev - ery peak and val - ley hum - ming With the Word, the Lord is

Peo-ple look East   and sing   to - day:

poco rall.

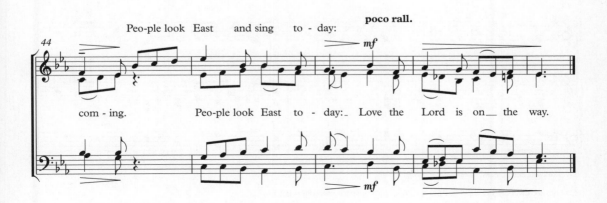

com - ing.   Peo-ple look East to - day:__ Love the Lord is on__ the way.

36. Prayer for the Blessing of Light

The Promise of His Glory

From 'Veni Emmanuel'
freely arranged by
MALCOLM ARCHER
(b. 1952)

Dynamics at performers' discretion.

37. Rejoice in the Lord alway

Philippians 4: 4–7

ANON. (mid-16th century, English)
edited by
Peter Le Huray
and David Willcocks

re - joice in the Lord___ al-way, and a-gain I say, re - joice,

re - joice in the Lord al-way, and a - gain I say,___ re-joice,

re - joice in the Lord al - way,___ and a-gain I say, re - joice, re-joice___

re - joice in the Lord al - way, and a-gain I say, re - joice, re -

re - joice in the Lord_____ al-way, and a-gain I say, re-joice,

re - joice, I say,___ re-joice, and a-gain I say, re-joice,

___ in the Lord___ al-way, in the Lord al - way, and a -

- joice in the Lord al - way, and a-gain I say, re-joice,

and a-gain I say, __ re - - joice. Let your

and a - gain I say, I say, re-joice. Let your

- gain I say, re-joice, and a - gain I say, re - - joice. Let your

and a-gain I say, re - joice, a - gain I say, re - joice. Let your

soft - ness be known un - to all men, let your soft - ness be known __ un - to all

soft - ness be known un - to all men, let your soft - ness be known __ un - to all

soft - ness be known un - to all men, let your soft - ness be known __ un - to all

soft - ness be known un - to all men, let your soft - ness be known __ un - to all

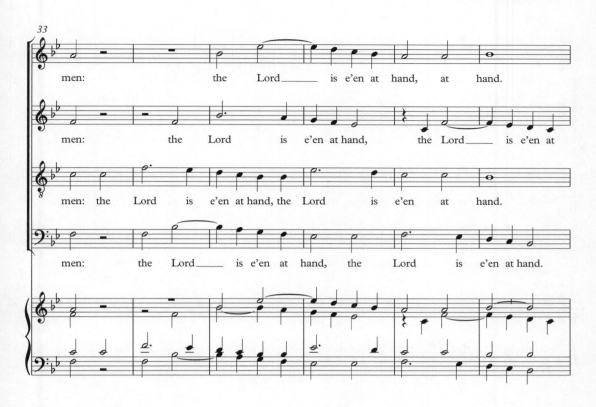

men: the Lord___ is e'en at hand, at hand.

men: the Lord is e'en at hand, the Lord___ is e'en at

men: the Lord is e'en at hand, the Lord is e'en at hand.

men: the Lord___ is e'en at hand, the Lord is e'en at hand.

Be care - ful___ for no - thing: but in all pray-er and sup-pli-ca-ti-

hand. Be care - ful for no - thing: but in all pray-er and sup-pli-ca-ti-

Be care - ful for no - thing: but in all pray-er and sup-pli-ca-ti-

Be care - ful for no - thing: but in all pray-er and sup-pli-ca-ti-

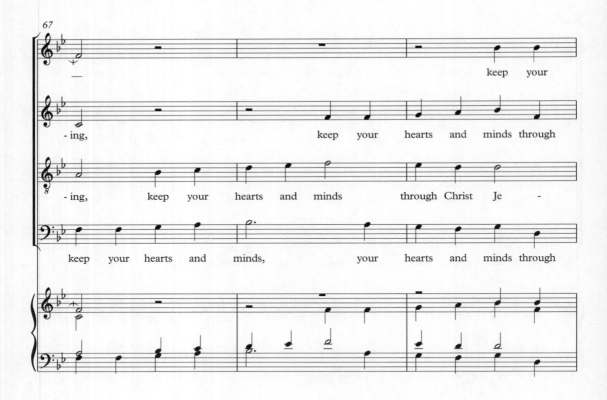

38. Remember, O thou man

Words: 16th-century English

THOMAS RAVENSCROFT
(*c*.1582–*c*.1635)

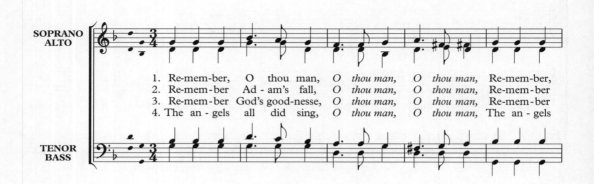

1. Re-mem-ber,   O   thou man,   *O thou man,*   *O thou man,*   Re-mem-ber,
2. Re-mem-ber   Ad - am's   fall,   *O thou man,*   *O thou man,*   Re-mem-ber
3. Re-mem-ber   God's good-nesse,   *O thou man,*   *O thou man,*   Re-mem-ber
4. The an - gels   all   did   sing,   *O thou man,*   *O thou man,*   The an - gels

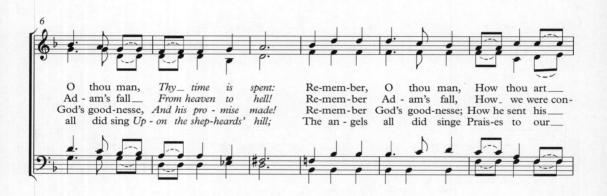

O thou man,   *Thy_ time is spent:*   Re-mem-ber,   O   thou man,   How thou art_
Ad - am's fall_   *From heaven to hell!*   Re-mem-ber   Ad - am's fall,   How_ we were con-
God's good-nesse,   *And his pro - mise made!*   Re-mem-ber   God's good-nesse;   How he sent his_
all   did sing *Up - on the shep-heards' hill;*   The an - gels   all   did singe Prais-es to our_

dead   and gone,   And   I   did   what   I   can: *There - fore re - pent!*
-dem - nëd all   In hell per - pe - tu - al,   *There for to dwell.*
Sonne, doubt-lesse,   Our sinnes for   to   re-dresse: *Be not af - fraid!*
heaven - ly King,   And peace to   man   liv - ing   *With a good will.*

39. The Angel Gabriel

Paraphrase by
Sabine Baring-Gould

Basque carol
arranged by
MALCOLM ARCHER
(b. 1952)

3. Then gen-tle Ma-ry meek-ly bowed her__ head,__ 'To me be as it pleas-eth

God',__ she said,__ 'My soul shall laud and mag-ni-fy his ho - ly__ name': Most

high-ly fa-voured la - dy. Glo - ri - a!

(ORG.)

Ped.

40. The Cherry Tree Carol

English traditional

arranged by
STEPHEN CLEOBURY
(b. 1948)

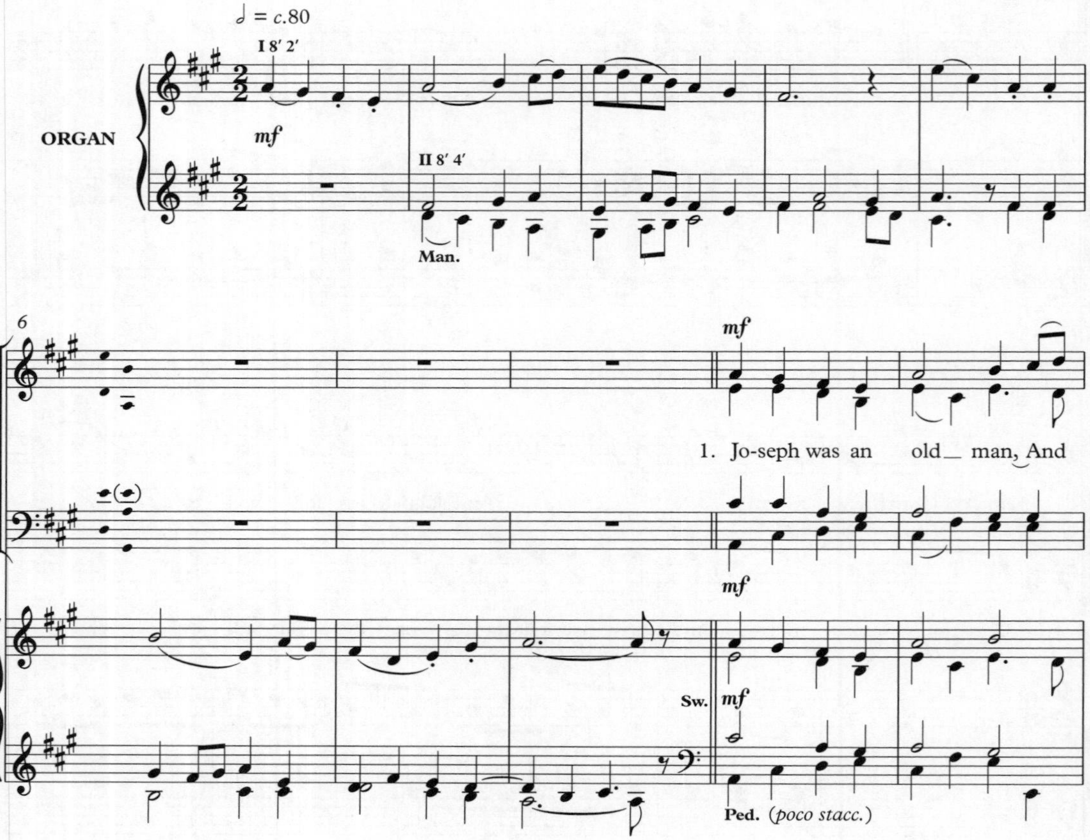

𝅗𝅥 = c.80
I 8′ 2′
ORGAN
mf
II 8′ 4′
Man.
6
S.
A.
T.
B.
mf
1. Jo-seph was an old_ man, And
mf
Sw.
mf
Ped. (poco stacc.)
11
an_ old_ man was he,___
When he wed-ded Ma - ry_ In the land of_ Ga - li -

3. O then be-spoke Ma - ry, So__ meek and__ O so mild,

'Pluck me one cher-ry, Jo - seph; For__ I am with__ child'.

Ah_____ ah____

Ah_____ ah_____

4. O then be-spoke Jo - seph, With words most__ un - kind,

Ah_____

'Let him pluck thee a cher - ry That brought thee with child'.   ah

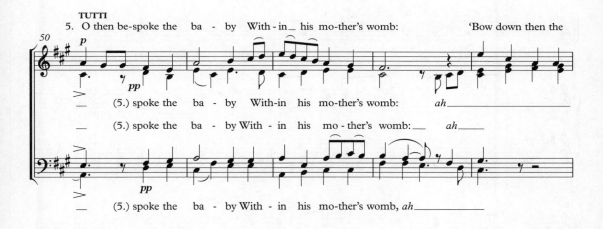

TUTTI

5. O then be-spoke the ba - by With - in his mo-ther's womb: 'Bow down then the

(5.) spoke the ba - by With-in his mo-ther's womb: ah

(5.) spoke the ba - by With - in his mo-ther's womb: ah

(5.) spoke the ba - by With - in his mo-ther's womb, ah

tall - est tree For my mo - ther to have some'.

SOPRANOS Semi-Chorus
6. Then bowed down the high-est tree Un - to his mo-ther's hand;

(ORG.)

SOLO II
Then she cried, 'See Jo - seph, I have cher-ries at com-mand'.

TENORS & BARITONES
7. O then be-spoke Jo - seph, 'I have done Ma-ry wrong; But cheer up my

76

dear - est, And be ye not cast down'.

mp legato
rit.

meno mosso

8. Then Ma - ry plucked a cher - ry, As_ red_ as_ a - ny

81

S.
A.

TUTTI   p

p

ah_____

T.
B.

p
ah_____

meno mosso

p

Ped. (+32')   (−32')

86   blood,

rit.
pp

_____ (8.) Then Ma - ry went she home - wards All_ with her hea - vy load.

pp

rit.

pp

Ped.   (+32')

for Bristol Cathedral Special Choir

41. The Linden Tree Carol

Translation by
George Ratcliffe Woodward
and others

MALCOLM ARCHER
(b. 1952)

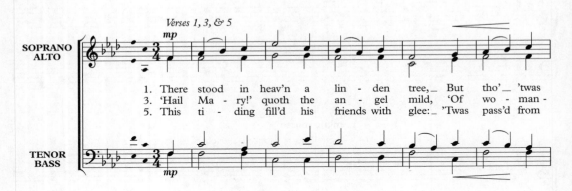

1. There stood in heav'n a lin - den tree, But tho' 'twas
3. 'Hail Ma - ry!' quoth the an - gel mild, 'Of wo - man
5. This ti - ding fill'd his friends with glee: 'Twas pass'd from

ho - ney - la - den, All an - gels cried, 'No bloom shall
- kind the fair - est: The Vir - gin ay shalt thou be
one to o - ther, 'Tis Ma - ry, see, And none but

after vv. 1 & 3: straight on for vv. 2 & 4

be Like that of one fair maid - en'.
styled, A babe al - though thou bear - est'.
she, And God will call her mo - ther.

Verses 2 & 4

2. Sped Ga - bri - el on wing - ed feet, And
4. 'So be___ it!' God's hand - maid - en cried, 'Ac -

pass'd___ through bolt - ed por - - tals, In
- cord - ing to thy tell - - ing.' Where -

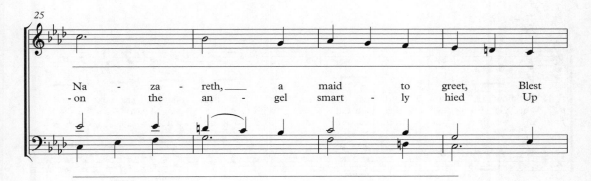

Na - za - reth,___ a maid to greet, Blest
- on the an - gel smart - ly hied Up

o'er___ all o - ther mor - - tals.
home - ward to___ his dwell - - ing.

42. There is a flow'r sprung of a tree

John Audelay

STANLEY VANN
(b. 1910)

The seed hereof was Godès sand** That God himself sowed
When that fair flow'r began to spread And his sweet blossom be-
with his hand,
-gan to bed†
(2.) In Nazareth, that holy land, Amidst her arbour a maiden
(4.) Then rich and poor of ev'ry land They marvell'd how this flow'r might

This bless-ed
Till king-ès }
found;   This } (2.) flow'r Sprang never but in Mary's bow'r.
spread,   Kings } (4.) three That bless-ed flow'r came to see.

Wansford, July 1992

* During Advent and festivals of the Blessed Virgin Mary, verses 4 and 5 may be omitted. The opening refrain may be repeated (after verse 3 of the shortened version and verse 5 of the full carol) a little slower and softer.

**sand = gift   †bed = bud

for Dr John Low Baldwin

43. There is no rose

Anonymous Medieval Carol

GERALD NEAR
(b. 1942)

There is no rose of such vir - tue_____ As is the

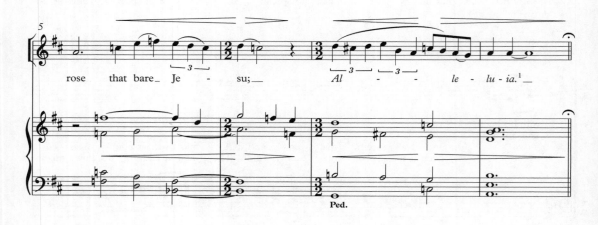

rose that bare_ Je - su;_ Al - - le - lu - ia.[1]_

For in this rose con-tain-ed was_____ Hea-ven and

[1] *Alleluia* = God be praised

Glo-ri - a in ex - cel - sis De - o:[4] ___ Gau - - de - a - mus.[5]

Poco meno mosso

S.
A.

Now leave we all this world-ly mirth, And fol-low we ___ this

T.
B.

Poco meno mosso

Man.

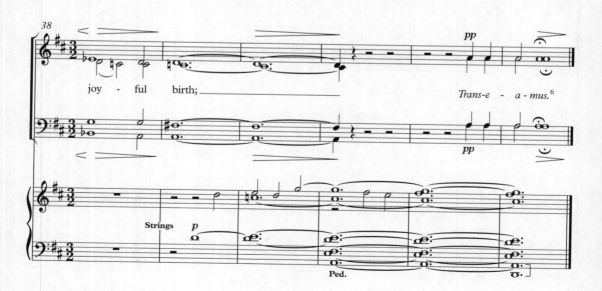

joy - ful birth; _____ Trans-e - a - mus.[6]

Strings

Ped.

[4]*Gloria in excelsis Deo* = Glory to God on high   [5]*Gaudeamus* = Let us rejoice   [6]*Transeamus* = Let us go

44. This is the record of John

John 1: 19

GRAYSTON IVES
(b. 1948)

Steady, flowing ($\quad$ = c.52)

like plainsong *

unis. *mp*

TENOR/
BASS

This is the re - cord of John, when the

ORGAN

p

Man.

Jews sent priests and Le - vites from Je - ru - sa - lem to ask him,

Fast, urgent ($\quad$ = c.116)

mf

f

S.
A.

'Who art thou, who art thou, who art thou?'

T.
B.

mf

f

Fast, urgent ($\quad$ = c.116)

---

* All the 'plainsong' passages to be sung quite freely.

45. This is the truth sent from above

English traditional

arranged by
R. VAUGHAN WILLIAMS
(1872–1958)

In performance the following scheme proves very effective: verse 1. Solo Soprano, verse 2. Solo Tenor/Baritone.   (The Editors)

Commissioned by the Dean and Chapter of Norwich Cathedral
for Michael Nicholas and the Cathedral Choir

46. Tomorrow go ye forth

Vesper Respond
Advent Sunday

GABRIEL JACKSON
(b. 1962)

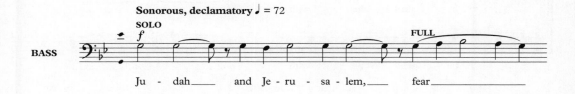

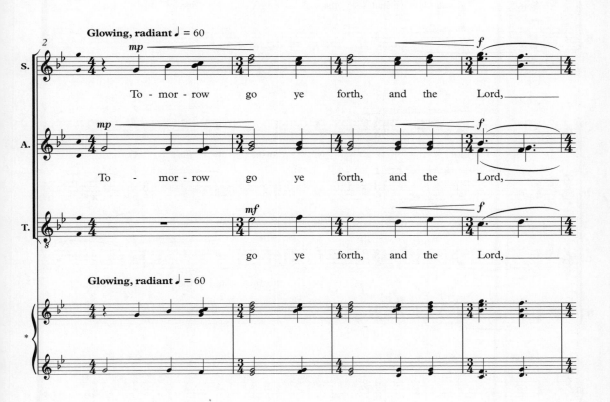

* Keyboard reduction for rehearsal only.

The companion Matin Respond 'I look from afar', also by Gabriel Jackson, is found on page 101 of this anthology.

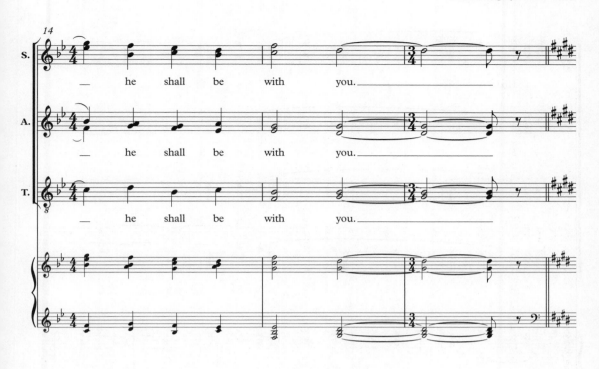

Ho - - - ly Spi - rit.

Ho - - - ly Spi - rit.

Ho - - - ly Spi - rit.

Ho - - - ly Spi - rit.

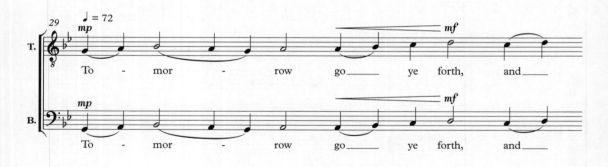

To - mor - row go___ ye forth, and___

To - mor - row go___ ye forth, and___

the Lord,___ he shall be with you.___

the Lord,___ he shall be with you.___

Baron's Court
5–15 November 1992

47. Veiled in darkness

Douglas Letel Rights

GLENN L. RUDOLPH
(b. 1951)

48. Vesper Responsory

G. P. da PALESTRINA (*c*.1525–94)
adapted by
PHILIP LEDGER (b. 1937)

Judah and Jerusalem, fear not, nor be dis-mayed;

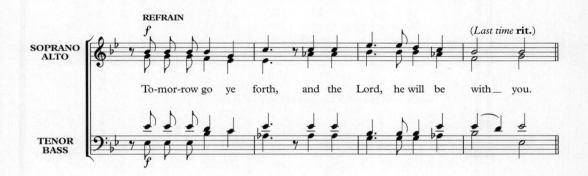

To-mor-row go ye forth, and the Lord, he will be with__ you.

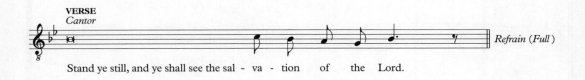

Stand ye still, and ye shall see the sal - va - tion of the Lord.

Glory be to the Fa-ther, and to the Son, and to the Ho-ly Ghost.

49. Virga Jesse floruit

(Out of Jesse springs a flower)

Alleluia verse at Feasts of the Virgin Mary
English version by John Rutter

ANTON BRUCKNER
(1824–96)
edited by
John Rutter

50. Wachet auf!

(*Wake, O wake!*)

Philipp Nicolai
translation by
Francis Crawford Birkitt

PHILIPP NICOLAI (1556–1608)
arranged by
J. S. BACH (1685–1750)

Original key C major.
Dynamics at performers' discretion.

13
hel— lem— Mun — de: 'Wo— seid ihr,— klu - gen
hear— them— say - ing; 'Where are— ye all,— ye
Wahr - heit mäch - tig: ihr— Licht— wird— hell, ihr
grace— un - end - ing! Her— light— shines— clear,— her

16
Jung - frau - en? Wohl auf,— der— Bräut - gam kommt; steht—
vir - gins wise? The Bride - groom— now— is— nigh: Stand—
Stern— geht auf!' Nun komm, du— wer - te— Kron, Herr—
star— a - scends. Ap - pear, thou pre - cious— Crown! God's—

19
auf,— die Lam - pen— nehmt! Hal - le - lu - ja! Macht euch be - reit zu
forth! your lamps raise— high! Ha - le - lu - ja! In bright ar - ray This—
Je - su, Gott - es— Sohn! Ho - si - an - na! Wir fol - gen all' zum
Son, to earth come down! Sing 'Ho - san - na!' Now rise we all To—

23
der— Hoch - zeit. Ihr— müs - set— ihm ent - ge - gen gehn!'
nup - tial day Go— forth— and— meet him in— the way!'
Freu - den - saal und— hal - ten— mit das A - bend - mal.
that— glad hall Where to— thy— feast thou dost us call.

Within an Advent Carol Service context, it may prove particularly effective for the whole chorale to be played on full organ while the choir moves from one part of the building to another. The choir then sings verse 1 unaccompanied and with great verve.

51. Wie soll ich dich empfangen

(How shall I fitly meet thee)

From The *Christmas Oratorio*

J. S. BACH
(1685–1750)
edited by
Malcolm Archer

Wie soll ich dich emp-fan- gen, und wie be- gegn ich dir?
O al- ler Welt Ver- lan- gen, o mei-ner See- len Zier!

How shall I fit - ly meet thee, And give thee wel - come due?
The na - tions long to greet thee, And I would greet thee too.

O Je - su, Je - su! set - ze mir selbst die Fa - ckel bei, da -
O Fount of Light, shine bright - ly Up - on my dark - en'd heart, That

-mit, was dich er - göt - ze, mir kund und wis - send sei.
I may serve thee right - ly, And know thee as thou art.

Dynamics at performers' discretion.

This piece may be performed accompanied or unaccompanied. If accompanied, the player should read the lower Bass part in bar 1 while the singers perform from the small notes an octave above. When unaccompanied, singers should use the lower Bass part to avoid the second inversion chord at the end of bar 1.

English translation reproduced by kind permission of Peters Edition Limited, London.

52. Zion, at thy shining gates

B. H. Kennedy

Melody: Bohemian Brethren (16th cent.)
arranged by
GEORGE GUEST
(b. 1924)

* This carol should be sung quickly, with a feeling of 1-in-the-bar, not 3.

hate.

T./B. *unis.* *mf*

Give   us   grace   thy   yoke   to   wear,   Give   us

mf

(Ped.)

T./B.

strength   thy   cross   to   bear,   Make   us   thine   in   deed   and

word,   Thine   in   heart   and   life,   O   Lord.

Great

APPENDIX

(Other suitable Advent music)

Abbreviations are used for the following, published or distributed by Oxford University Press:

Anthems for Choirs 4	*AfC 4*
Carols for Choirs	*CfC (2 or 3)*
Church Music Society	*CMS*
100 Carols for Choirs	*100 CfC*
European Sacred Music	*ESM*
The New Church Anthem Book	*NCAB*
The Oxford Book of Tudor Anthems	*OBTA*
The Shorter New Oxford Book of Carols	*SNOBC*
Tudor Church Music Series	*TCM*

Titles also available as separate leaflets are listed below as: *OUP*

Pieces suitable for unaccompanied singing are marked thus *.

TITLE	COMPOSER / ARRANGER / EDITOR	SOURCE
General repertoire		
Any setting of the Ave Maria		
Any setting of the Benedictus		
Any setting of the Magnificat		
Specific repertoire		
* Adam lay ybounden	Boris Ord	*CfC 2; SNOBC*
Adam lay ybounden	Peter Warlock	*100 CfC; OUP*
* Arise, shine	G. L. Rudolph	*OUP*
* A spotless Rose	Herbert Howells	*100 CfC*
And the glory of the Lord	G. F. Handel ed. Bartlett	*Messiah* (OUP edition)
Angelus ad virginem	arr. Willcocks	*CfC 3; 100 CfC*
* Audivi Media nocte	Thomas Tallis ed. Le Huray & Willcocks	*A Sixteenth-Century Anthem Book*
* Ave Maria	Josquin Desprez ed. Rutter	*ESM*
* Ave Maria	Robert Parsons ed. Steinitz / ed. Milsom	*OBTA; TCM*
* Ave Maria	Igor Stravinsky	*ESM*
* Bogoroditsye Dyevo	Sergei Rachmaninov	*ESM*
Christ's Love-song	Francis Grier	*OUP*
* Dixit Maria	H. L. Hassler ed. Rutter	*ESM*
* Gabriel's Message	arr. Willcocks	*CfC 2*
* Let us sing with gladness	Mendelssohn ed. Marlow	*CMS:* from *Six Seasonal Motets*
* Lift up your heads	Orlando Gibbons ed. Morehen	*TCM*
* God so loved the world	John Stainer	*Ash Wednesday to Easter for Choirs*

* God so loved the world	Bob Chilcott	*Ash Wednesday to Easter for Choirs*; OUP
* Hail! Blessed Virgin Mary	Charles Wood	*CfC 2; 100 CfC*
* Hosanna to the Son of David	Orlando Gibbons ed. Greening	*OBTA; TCM*
* Hosanna to the Son of David	Thomas Weelkes ed. Morehen	*OBTA; TCM*
How beautiful are the feet	G. F. Handel ed. Bartlett	*Messiah* (OUP edition)
I sing of a Maiden	Patrick Hadley	*CfC 2*
* Laetentur coeli	William Byrd ed. Gardner / ed. Bray / ed. Symons	*A Cappella; OBTA; TCM*
* Laetentur coeli	Michael Berkeley	from *Eight Motets*
* Let all mortal flesh keep silence	Edward C. Bairstow	*AfC 4*
Lift up your heads	G. F. Handel ed. Bartlett	*Messiah* (OUP edition)
Lift up your heads	arr. Willcocks	*OUP*
Never weather-beaten sail	Charles Wood	*NCAB*
Nova, nova	Grayston Ives	*OUP*
O come, O come, Emmanuel	Andrew Carter	*OUP*
* Out of your sleep	Richard Rodney Bennett	*CfC 2; 100 CfC*
Rejoice in the Lord, alway	Henry Purcell ed. Wood / ed. Watkins Shaw	*A Purcell Anthology; CMS; NCAB*
* Richte mich, Gott	Felix Mendelssohn	*ESM*
* Rorate caeli desuper	William Byrd ed. Milsom	*TCM*
* The angel Gabriel from heaven came	arr. Pettman	*SNOBC*
The Lord at first did Adam make	arr. Cleobury	*OUP*
The Lord at first did Adam make	arr. Willcocks	*CfC 2; OUP*
The Lord will surely come	Gerre Hancock	*OUP*
The Song of the Tree of Life	R. Vaughan Williams	*OUP*
Their sound is gone out	G. F. Handel ed. Bartlett	*Messiah* (OUP edition)
There is no rose	Benjamin Britten	*CfC 3*
* There is no rose of such virtue	John Joubert	*SNOBC*
This is the record of John	Orlando Gibbons ed. Le Huray	*NCAB; OBTA; TCM*
* Thou knowest, Lord	Henry Purcell ed. Wood / ed. Hogwood	*A Purcell Anthology; NCAB; Funeral Sentences*
Thou wilt keep him in perfect peace	S. S. Wesley	*NCAB*
* Vigilate	William Byrd ed. Morehen	*TCM*
We wait for Thy loving kindness	William McKie	*AfC 4; OUP*
Zion hears the watchmen's voices	J. S. Bach ed. Rutter	*CfC 2; OUP*